I0766477

Please leave your name and comment below

Please leave your name and comment below

Please leave your name and comment below

Please leave your name and comment below

Please leave your name and comment below

Please leave your name and comment below

Please leave your name and comment below

Please leave your name and comment below

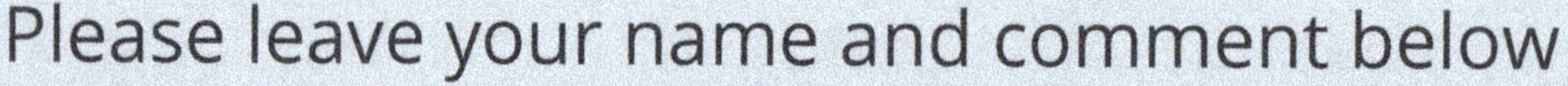

Please leave your name and comment below

Please leave your name and comment below

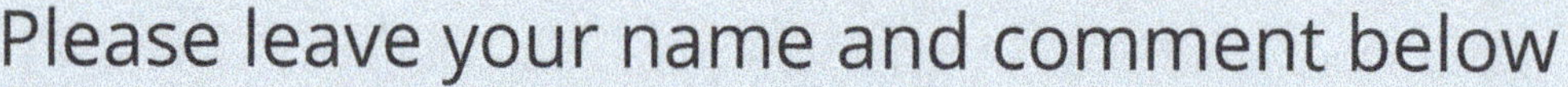

Please leave your name and comment below

Please leave your name and comment below

Please leave your name and comment below

Please leave your name and comment below

Please leave your name and comment below

Please leave your name and comment below

Please leave your name and comment below

Please leave your name and comment below

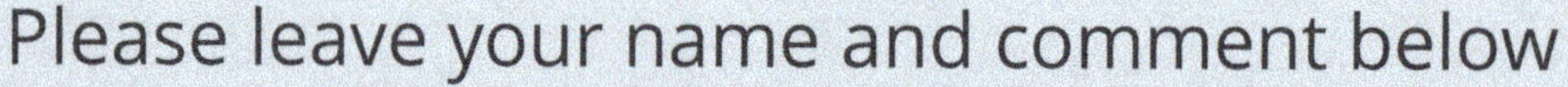

Please leave your name and comment below

Please leave your name and comment below

Please leave your name and comment below

Please leave your name and comment below

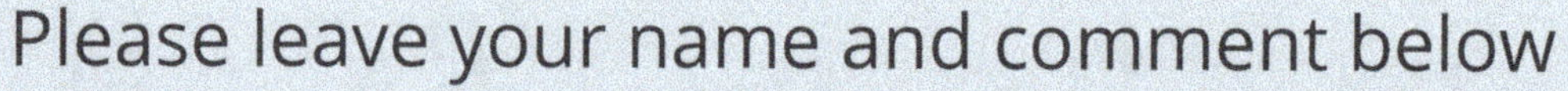
Please leave your name and comment below

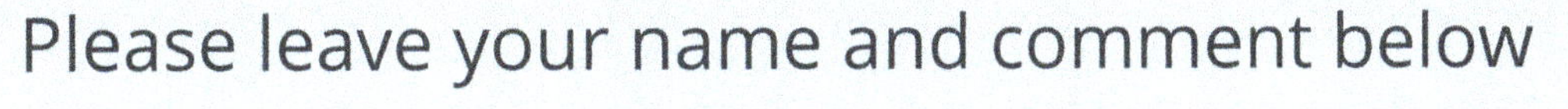

Please leave your name and comment below

Please leave your name and comment below

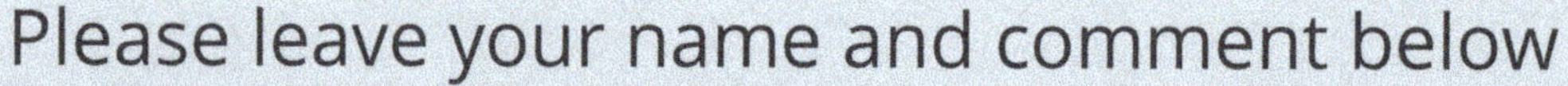

Please leave your name and comment below

Please leave your name and comment below

Please leave your name and comment below

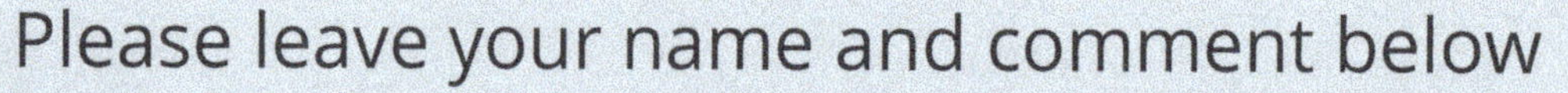

Please leave your name and comment below

Please leave your name and comment below

Please leave your name and comment below

Please leave your name and comment below

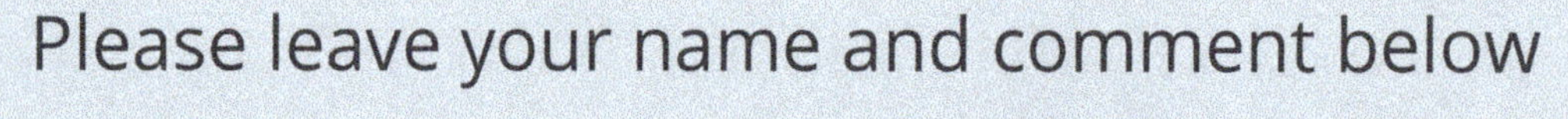

Please leave your name and comment below

Please leave your name and comment below

Please leave your name and comment below

Please leave your name and comment below

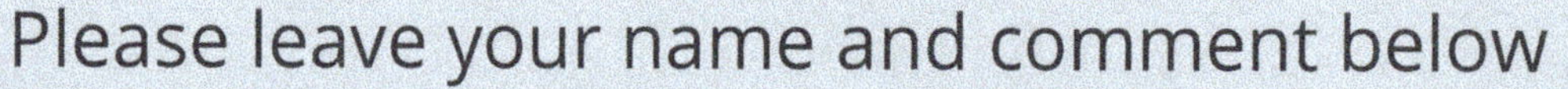

Please leave your name and comment below

Please leave your name and comment below

Please leave your name and comment below

Gift Log

Gift Log

Gift Log

Gift Log

Gift Log

Gift Log

Gift Log

Gift Log

www.ingramcontent.com/pod-product-compliance
Lightning Source LLC
Chambersburg PA
CBHW041157300726
48981CB00004B/280